节气之美

五感六觉中品味时间

Beauty of Solar Terms:
Tasting Time Through Human Senses and Feelings

北京师范大学出版集团
BEIJING NORMAL UNIVERSITY PUBLISHING GROUP
北京师范大学出版社

图书在版编目（CIP）数据

节气之美：五感六觉中品味时间 / 王立刚主编. ——
北京：北京师范大学出版社, 2019.11
（大美系列丛书 / 于丹主编）
ISBN 978-7-303-24497-3

Ⅰ.①节… Ⅱ.①王… Ⅲ.①节气–风俗习惯–中国
–通俗读物 Ⅳ.①K892.18-49

中国版本图书馆CIP数据核字(2018)第292945号

营 销 中 心 电 话 010–58805072 58807651
北师大出版社高等教育与学术著作分社 http://xueda.bnup.com

出版发行：北京师范大学出版社 www.bnup.com
　　　　　北京市西城区新街口外大街12-3号
　　　　　邮政编码：100088
印　　刷：北京盛通印刷股份有限公司
经　　销：全国新华书店
开　　本：787 mm×1092 mm　1/16
印　　张：10
字　　数：155千字
版　　次：2019年11月第1版
印　　次：2019年11月第1次印刷
定　　价：48.00元

策划编辑：王则灵　　　　　责任编辑：王　宁
美术编辑：李向昕　　　　　装帧设计：水长流文化
责任校对：段立超　　　　　责任印制：马　洁

序

　　我喜欢一切带着时光打磨痕迹的东西，比如水滴滑过墙，浸润墙体的驳杂，滋润苔藓；比如风绕过老树，老树皮里藏着不动声色的年轮；再比如一遍遍鞣过的皮子，越来越贴近人的皮肤质感；还有像莱昂纳德·科恩那样的老乐手，鬓染霜华，用沙哑的老灵魂唱着自己的诗和歌。时光打磨的痕迹，不止褶皱，还有润泽。我们的今生不过是从岁月里借来了一把光阴，冠上自己的名字，走自己人生的节序如流。

　　在西方讲学的时候，曾经被问到中国的节日和西方的节日到底有什么差别？我半开玩笑地说，西方的节日特点很明显，复活节、感恩节，几乎所有节日都是人给神过的，是向神灵致敬；然而中国却不一样，从春节到清明，再到端午、中秋、重阳，绝大部分是为人而过，追慕人的精神家园，是给人过的节。从小进教堂的人习惯于孤单而优美、崇高而持久地膜拜天上下来的神；而中国人，应时而动，顺应自然，春暖以生，夏暑以养，秋清以杀，冬寒以藏。

　　中国人的记忆里，会萦绕着童声朗朗的念诵："春雨惊春清谷天，夏满芒夏暑相连，秋处露秋寒霜降，冬雪雪冬小大寒……"《二十四节气歌》，是一首四季变换的歌，有图有景，有颜色，有味道。中国人解释立春——东风解冻，蛰虫始振，鱼陟负冰；立夏——蝼蝈鸣，蚯蚓出，阴气始而二物应之；立秋——凉风至，白露降，寒蝉鸣；立冬——终也，万物收藏也。这是多有诗意的描述。

　　二十四节气，通贯我们的一生，年复一年，流光被打上了烙印。这样接地气的日子，人们才过得踏实。

于丹

二十四节气歌

清代王用臣

薛琴访增补

春雨惊春清谷天，夏满芒夏暑相连。

秋处露秋寒霜降，冬雪雪冬小大寒。

每月两节不变更，最多相差一两天。

上半年逢六廿一，下半年逢八廿三。

  二十四节气是中国古人发明的岁时纪年方法。人们利用土圭实测太阳投射到物体上的影子，依据影子的长短、方向的改变，将一年分为了二十四个节气，为每个节气总结出一些典型特征，用以指导农业生产，开展文化活动。

  最初，二十四节气的名称和内容主要反映黄河流域的物候和天气特征。在历史发展过程中，二十四节气的文化内涵越来越丰富，其影响也扩展到中华文化圈的各个地区，构成了中国文化的重要组成部分。

  按照阳历看，一年二十四节气中，上半年（1—6月）的节气在每月的6日、21日前后，下半年（7—12月）的节气在每月的8日、23日前后。

  一年二十四个节气，体现了一年的节令变化和文化习俗。

目录

惠崇春江晚景（其一）

苏轼

竹外桃花三两枝，春江水暖鸭先知。

菱蒿满地芦芽短，正是河豚欲上时。

春生

1. 立春

每年二月上旬进入立春，立春是二十四节气中的第一个节气。

东风解冻，蛰虫始振，鱼陟负冰。

——《月令七十二候集解》

东风：古人以东风代指温暖的春风。

蛰（zhé）：冬眠。

陟（zhì）：上升。

　　二十四节气中有立春、立夏、立秋、立冬四个节气，其中"立"是"开始"的意思。

　　立春前后，我国北方的气候乍暖还寒，刺骨的寒风逐渐消散，天寒地冻的场景逐步改变，冬眠的动物就要醒来，潜在河里的鱼也开始想要浮到水面上来透透气。

3

听

鸟鸣

顾况在《山径柳》中这样描述道："宛转若游丝，浅深栽绿崦。年年立春后，即被啼莺占。"声声鸟鸣，叫醒了沉睡的人，也唤醒了沉睡的大地。春天的乐章就这样开始了。

嗅

梅花

在古代，梅与松、竹并称为"岁寒三友"，是冬日里陪伴人们的植物。宋代王安石写下《梅花》这首诗："墙角数枝梅，凌寒独自开。遥知不是雪，为有暗香来。"在严寒时节，梅花率先开放，其高洁、坚强的品格，一直为文人雅士所称赞。

春饼

立春前后，很多地区流行吃春饼、春卷等节令食品。春饼是一种烫面薄饼，用热水和面，分成两小块儿面团，面团中间抹油，擀成薄饼，烙熟后卷菜吃。

唐代的《四时宝镜》记载："立春，食芦、春饼、生菜，号'菜盘'。"可见，春饼至少已经有一千多年的历史了。

鞭春牛

旧时，立春前有鞭春牛的习俗。人们用土做成牛的形状，称为"春牛"。在祭坛上举行祭祀活动之后，人们会手执柳条鞭打"春牛"，同时口喊道：一打风调雨顺，二打国泰民安，三打五谷丰登等吉祥话。很多地区会将"春牛"打碎，人人争抢碎土，称为"抢春"，还会将抢到的碎土带回家，撒在牛栏内，祈望自家牲畜能够健康。

知 💡

"春"字的结构，上边是"艹"字头，表示草木生长，中间是"屯"字，下边为"日"，表示春阳抚照，万物滋荣。

- 书中提到"鞭春牛"，为什么选择牛这种动物作为立春庆祝活动的对象？
- 立春的"立"是什么意思？

1. The beginning of Spring

The beginning of Spring, the first solar term, is in the first ten days of February.

👁 Seeing

After this solar term, It becomes warmer and warmer in North China.The cold wind will disappear, and the hibernating animals will wake up later. The fish in the river comes to the surface just for the fresh air.

👂 Listening

Around the beginning of Spring, the birds' singing wakes everything up, Spring is coming.

👃 Smelling

The plum, pine and bamboo are known as "the three companions in winter", which can accompany people in cold winter.

👄 Eating

Around the beginning of the spring, Spring Pancakes are popular in many places. The Spring Pancake is very thin, and popular for over one thousand years.

✋ Touching

It's a custom to whip the cattle around this solar term. While People is doing the whipping action, they are also shouting: whipping the cattle the first time is for good weather for the corps.

2·雨水

每年二月下旬进入雨水，雨水是二十四节气的第二个节气。

视

天一生水，獭祭鱼，候雁北。

——《月令七十二候集解》

天一生水：古人认为，水是万物的本源。明代著名的藏书楼"天一阁"，名称便取自"天一生水"，可以避免火灾的意思。

獭祭鱼：獭喜欢吃鱼，常将捕到的鱼放在岸边，古人认为似乎是在陈列祭品，便称之为"獭祭鱼"或"獭祭"。

雁：一种候鸟。

雨水，意味着降水的开始。天气慢慢回暖，北方一般不再下雪，而是开始下雨。雨水前后，北方的大多数植物开始返青。

听

雨声

　　春天的雨经常是静悄悄的，"随风潜入夜，润物细无声"。不过，有时候也会出现"夜来风雨声，花落知多少"的情况，不期而至的春雨还带落了些许春天的花朵。

嗅

迎春花

　　迎春花的绽放预示着春天的到来，黄色的小花，一片一片，富有暖意。

味

春笋

春笋号称"素食第一品"，自古以来便备受人们喜爱。白居易写过《食笋》诗，其中便有"此处乃竹乡，春笋满山谷；山夫折盈抱，抱来早市鬻。"（鬻yù，卖的意思。）

你知道哪些用春笋做的菜肴呢？

触

春雨

在农业社会，人们对雨水这个节气有着很深刻的感触。俗话说："立春雨水到，早起晚睡觉。"雨水前后，冬小麦自南向北开始返青，忙碌的田间管理就要开始，而这一时期的雨水也显得特别宝贵，雨水节气下雨是风调雨顺的象征，所谓"雨水有雨庄稼好，大春小春一片宝。"正是如此。

11

"雨"字是象形字，上边的"一"表示"天"，下边的"冂"表示"云"，中间的四点表示落下的雨水。

· 你知道哪些用春笋做的菜肴呢？

· 为什么说"春雨贵如油"？

2. Corn Rain

Corn Rain, the second solar term, is in the last ten days of February.

👁 Seeing

Corn Rain marks the beginning of rainy days. It starts to become warmer and it doesn't snow in the North. During these days, all the plants turn to green.

👂 Listening

It often rains quietly in spring, but sometimes people can hear the rain and it can blow down the flowers at night.

👃 Smelling

The bloom of winter jasmine heralds the arrival of spring. Its yellow flowers symbolize warmth.

👄 Eating

In spring, the bamboo is a kind of nutritionally enriched vegetables and people like it very much. Do you know which dishes are made of bamboo?

✋ Touching

In agriculture society, Corn Rain has a deep impression on people. During these days, the wheat turns to green from the South to the North. The busy work in the fields will begin, so the rain is very precious. The rain these days means the wind and rain come in their time.

3. 惊蛰

每年三月上旬进入惊蛰，惊蛰是二十四节气中的第三个节气。

视 👁

万物出乎震，震为雷，故曰惊蛰，是蛰虫惊而出走矣。

——《月令七十二候集解》

14

注解

震：此处代表雷声阵阵，唤醒万物。

解读

　　惊蛰前后，天气变暖，北方很多植物即将开花，冬眠的动物醒来开始活动。惊蛰之后，暖空气活动频繁，加大了空气的不稳定性，我国南方大部分地区春雷滚滚。

春雷滚滚

"惊雷奋兮震万里，威凌宇宙兮动四海。"《惊雷歌》中的话描述了春天的雷声唤醒万物的情景。

杏花

杏花、梨花、桃花先后开放。你能分清楚这几种花吗？

惊蛰食梨

民间素有"惊蛰食梨"的习俗。惊蛰前后，天气一般比较干燥，乍暖还寒，容易使人感到口干，吃梨可以生津止渴，而"梨"与"犁"谐音，春耕大多在此期间展开，食梨也寄托了人们希望一年生活顺利的美好愿望。

"打小人"

惊蛰前后，各种虫子即将开始活动。生活在农村的人为了减少虫子带来的疾病，在惊蛰当日会手持艾草等香草，借助其特殊的味道赶跑虫。后来，这种做法在某些地方变成了"打小人"的习俗，人们会在这一天拍打纸做的小人，用以驱赶生活中的霉运。

"蛰"字是形声字，"执"为声旁，"虫"为形旁，表示动物藏起来冬眠。惊蛰，意为惊醒了正在冬眠的虫子。

· 你能分清楚杏花、梨花、桃花这几种花吗？

· "春日农家闲不住，赶马牵牛耕作忙"，描写的是哪一个节气？

3. Awakening from Hibernation

Awakening from Hibernation, the third solar term, is in the first ten days of March.

👁 Seeing

Around this solar term, many plants in the North will bloom and the animals in hibernation will wake up. After the solar term, the warm air moves frequently, which increases the instability of the air. People in the South can hear the sound of thunder rolling.

👂 Listening

The thunder in spring waken thousands of plants and animals.

👃 Smelling

The flowers of apricot, pear and peach bloom one after another. Can you tell the differences between them?

👄 Eating

It's a custom to eat pears these days. It is very dry and getting warmer, so people tend to feel thirsty. Pears are rich in water, in addition, the Chinese Character's sound of pears is the same as the character's sound of plough. The plough work starts in this period and eating pears is a symbol of a lucky life in the year.

✋ Touching

During the days around this solar term, all kinds of insects become to be active. The people in the countryside use the warmwood or other plants full of fragrance to repel the insects and mouses in order to reduce the disease caused by them. Later, this practice becomes a custom named "beating the paper man" for avoiding the bad things.

4. 春分

每年三月下旬进入春分，春分是二十四节气中的第四个节气。

视

分者，半也，此当九十日之半，故谓之分……春分正阴阳适中，故昼夜无长短，云元鸟至。

——《月令七十二候集解》

20

九十日：如果将一年平分为四季，每季大约为九十日。

元鸟：燕子。

　　春分当天，昼夜平分，古人认为这是一个阴阳平衡的时节。春分之后，阳气就开始胜过阴气，北方的杨树、柳树开始发芽变绿，出外踏青的时节到了。

燕子声

"呢喃燕子语梁间，底事来惊梦里闲。"

嗅

海棠

　　"偷来梨蕊三分白，借得梅花一缕魂。"曹雪芹在《红楼梦》里假林黛玉之口这样描述春天的海棠花。海棠花一般没有香味，但西府海棠却既香且艳，是海棠中的上品。

味

春菜

　　岭南地区有"春分吃春菜"的习俗，将采回的春菜与鱼片"滚汤"，名曰"春汤"。有顺口溜道："春汤灌脏，洗涤肝肠。阖家老少，平安健康。"

23

立春蛋

民间有句俗语："春分到，蛋儿俏。"春分这一天最好玩的莫过于"竖蛋"，也称"春分立蛋"。这是一个流传很久的游戏。

在春分这一天，找一枚鸡蛋，尝试一下看看在平整的桌面上能不能将其竖起来吧。

"分"字下边为"刀"，上边为"八"。"八"字的字形也是"分开"的意思，"分"表示"刀以分别物也"，进而引申为"平分"的意思。

- 在春分这一天，找一枚鸡蛋，尝试一下看看在平整的桌面上能不能将其竖起来吧。
- "吃了春分饭，一天长一线"是什么意思？

4. Spring Equinox

春分

Spring Equinox, the fourth solar term, is in the last ten days of March.

Seeing

Equinox means half. There are four seasons in a year, and each season has about ninety days. On Spring Equinox, the day and night are of equal length. The ancients think it is a time of balance between Yin and Yang. After this solar term, Yang begins to be over than Yin. The willow trees in the North begin to sprout and turn green. It's time to go out.

Listening

People can hear the singing of the swallow.

Smelling

In general, Chinese flowering crab-apple don't have fragrance. Only XIFU crab-apple, the best kind of Chinese flowering crab-apple, smells sweet and is colourful.

Eating

It's a custom to eat the spring vegetables in Lingnan area. There is a famous soup made with spring vegetables and fish. This soup is nutritious and suitable for all ages.

Touching

There is a game that has been popular for a long time, which is called "standing egg".

Please find an egg during this period, and try to let the egg stand on a flat table.

5·清明

每年四月上旬进入清明，清明是二十四节气中的第五个节气。

视

物至此时皆以洁齐而清明矣。桐始华，田鼠化为鴽，虹始见。

——《月令七十二候集解》

26

化为鴽（rú）：指田鼠像小
鸟一样多了起来。

　　清明是重要的节气，也是我国重要的传
统节日。清明前后，阳光和煦，春风荡漾，
花红柳绿，气清景明。清明节是出外踏青插
柳、祭祀祖先的日子。

黄鹂

"两个黄鹂鸣翠柳，一行白鹭上青天。"黄鹂是古诗中经常出现的鸟，其清脆婉转的鸣声，是春天的象征，让人愉悦。

梧桐

清明前后，梧桐花开放。梧桐是古诗中常出现的树，如"无言独上西楼，月如钩。寂寞梧桐深院锁清秋。"

青团

　　在南方，清明节有吃青团的习俗。将名叫"浆麦草"的植物捣烂，拌入糯米粉中，作成青绿色的团子，蒸熟后糯韧绵软，清香扑鼻。不少地区也用青团来祭祀祖先。

放风筝

　　俗语说："杨柳青，放风筝。"清明节前后是北方放风筝的时节，因此时惠风习习，而且天气大多晴朗，适合放风筝。

　　同时，清明也是重要的传统节日。在清明节期间，人们多会出外扫墓、踏青，各地拥有丰富多彩的活动。

"清"字的偏旁为三点水，早期表示水的纯净透明，后来引申为干净。"清明"本是天朗气清的意思。我国清明时节并非处处都是天朗气清的天气，"清明"一词是一种美好的希望。

· 你见过的风筝，都有哪些形状和造型？

· 清明节扫墓，是为了什么？

5. Clear and Bright

Clear and Bright, the fifth solar term, is in the first ten days of April.

Seeing

Clear and Bright is an important solar term, as well as an important traditional Chinese festival. During this period, the sun shines warmly. The wind is soft. The flowers are red and the willows are green. Cleaning the tombs and paying respect to the dead with offerings are the two important activities in this solar term. It is not only a period for commemorating the dead, but also It's the time for people to go out and enjoy nature.

Listening

The oriole is a birdwhich often appears in ancient poetry. The clear sound of this bird is the symbol of spring and can make people happy.

Smelling

Around this solar term, the Wutong trees' flowers bloom.

Eating

In the South it's a custom to eat green dumplings. The making procedure is, first we should mash a plant called "wheat straw pulp" , and then we mix it with glutinous rice flour. At last we make it like green dumplings. This food tastes glutinous and fragrant. In many areas this food is also used to worship the ancestors.

Touching

Around this solar term, it is suitable for flying kites. Flying kites is a popular game at this time in a year.

6. 谷雨

每年四月下旬进入谷雨，谷雨是二十四节气中的第六个节气。

自雨水后，土膏脉动，今又雨，其谷于水也。萍始生，鸣鸠拂其羽。

——《月令七十二候集解》

注解

土膏：土地中的养分。唐代皇甫冉《杂言无锡惠山寺流泉歌》回："土膏脉动知春早，隈奥阴深长苔草。"

萍：浮萍，一年生草本植物，浮生水面，叶子扁平，表面绿色，背面紫红色，叶下生须根，开白花。

鸣鸠（jiū）：布谷鸟。

解读

谷雨时节，气候转暖，桃花竞相开放，布谷鸟啼鸣，这是播种移苗、点豆种瓜的最佳时节，也是户外活动的最佳时节。

布谷鸟

"万壑树参天，千山响杜鹃。"布谷鸟又称杜鹃、子规，春夏之交常在我国南方活动，进入夏季后会来到北方，声音响亮清脆，因其叫声音似"布谷"，故而得名。

槐花

槐花盛开，满城飘香。槐树是我国北方最常见的树种之一，它所盛开的槐花，具有淡淡的、甜甜的味道。

味

香椿

　　俗话说："雨前香椿嫩如丝。"此处，"雨"即指谷雨。谷雨前后正是香椿上市的时节。嫩香椿叶醇香爽口，营养价值高。

　　与香椿相对应的一种树是臭椿，古代称香椿为"椿"，称臭椿为"樗"，你能分得清香椿和臭椿吗？

触

谷雨茶

　　谷雨茶，是在谷雨时节采制的茶，又叫二春茶。

山谷的"谷"与作为粮食的"谷"在古代是两个字。谷雨的"谷"字取意后者，在古代的写法为"穀"，形声字，由"禾""殳"两部分组成，是庄稼和粮食的总称。

- 香椿和臭椿的区别是什么？
- 在节气里，"雨水"和"谷雨"的雨有什么区别？

6. Grain Rain

Grain Rain, the sixth solar term, is in the last ten days of April.

 Seeing

It's very warm during this solar term. The peach flowers blossom and the cuckoo sing. It's time to plant beans and sow the seeds. It's also the best time for outdoor activities.

Listening

At the turning of spring and summer, cuckoos often sing in the South. After entering the summer, they come to the North. The sound of the cuckoo is loud and clear. The bird is just named after its sound.

Smelling

The kowhai tree is one of the most common trees in North China. The light and sweet flavor of the kowhai tree has accompanied many people.

Eating

It's time to eat toona sinensis during these days. The leaves of toona sinensis are very delicious and have high nutritional value.

There is another tree called Ailanthus Altissima. Can you tell the difference between toona sinensis and ailanthus altissima?

Touching

It rains a lot in the South during these days and drinking tea at this time are good for health.

山亭夏日

高骈

绿树阴浓夏日长，楼台倒影入池塘。

水晶帘动微风起，满架蔷薇一院香。

夏长

7. 立夏

每年五月上旬进入立夏，立夏是二十四节气中的第七个节气。

视

夏，假也，物至此时皆假大也。蝼蝈鸣，蚯蚓出，阴气始而二物应之。

——《月令七十二候集解》

蝼蝈（lóu guō）：青蛙的古
称，《礼记·月令》："蝼蝈
鸣，蚯蚓出。"郑玄注曰："蝼
蝈，蛙也。"一说"蝼蝈"为
"蝼蛄（gū）"，昆虫，褐
色，有翅，咬食农作物的根，亦
称"天蝼"。

　　立夏以后，我国南北方的气温
都开始上升，南方尤其明显。北方
的小麦开始长出麦穗，田间的害虫
也多了起来。

蝼蝈鸣

"草根蝼蝈鸣，湖上兼葭靡。"此处蝼蝈指蝼蛄，咬食农作物的根部，是一种对农作物有害的昆虫。

丁香

立夏前后，正是丁香花最盛的时节，远远就能闻到浓郁的花香。在文学作品中，"丁香"是忧郁情节的代名词，如李商隐的"芭蕉不展丁香结，同向春风各自愁。"

立夏饭

　　古时候，人们在立夏时节，用赤豆、黄豆、黑豆、青豆、绿豆五色豆与粳米一起，煮成"五色饭"，称为"立夏饭"。有的地方会摘食时新的水果蔬菜，称为"立夏尝新"。

"秤人"

　　南方一带有立夏秤人的习俗。长辈们在院内竖起大秤，男女老幼依次称一称体重。因为炎热的夏天容易令人食欲不振、体重减轻。所以，以前的人们往往会将数字多报一些，求取吉利。

"夏"字是象形字，上边是"页"（xié），中间是"臼"（jù），下边是"夊"（suī）。页表示"头部"。"臼"表示两只手，夊表示"两足"，合起来为人的身体形状。《说文解字》认为："夏，中国之人也。"

· 华夏民族的"夏"字是什么意思？

7. Start of Summer

Start of Summer, the seventh solar term, is in the first ten days of May.

👁 Seeing

After the Start of Summer, the temperature becomes higher both in the South and North in China, especially in the South. The plants and grain begin to grow quickly at this time. There are more pests in the field.

👂 Listening

People can hear grasshoppers at this time.

👃 Smelling

Around the Start of Summer, it is the most prosperous season of lilacs. People can smell the fragrance far away.

👄 Eating

People often eat the "Summer Meal"on this solar term,which is made by adzukis, soybeans, black beans' mung beans and rice. In some places, people also pick up the fresh fruits and vegetables to make the meal.

✋ Touching

It's a custom to weighing people in the South. The elder people put a scale in the yard and every person in the family should weigh. People always eat less in the hot summer and their weight will reduce. So, people in the past tended to give a higher weight for luck.

8.小满

每年五月下旬进入小满，小满是二十四节气中的第八个节气。

视

小满者，物至于此小得盈满。苦菜秀，靡草死，麦秋至。

——《月令七十二候集解》

46

苦菜：一种野菜，菊科苦菜属，多生于路旁荒地等处，嫩苗可食用。

　　小满时节，北方地区小麦等夏熟农作物籽粒开始饱满，麦收的季节就要到了；而南方则进入多雨的季节。

听

画眉鸟

　　"百啭千声随意移，山花红紫树高低。始知锁向金笼听，不及林间自在啼。"入夏前后，是画眉鸟繁殖的季节。画眉鸟的叫声高亢激昂、婉转多变。

嗅

枣花

　　小满前后，我国北方很多花进入花期，其中枣花是重要的蜜源。这一时期采得的枣花蜂蜜口感好，更受蜂蜜爱好者的青睐。

苦苦菜

苦苦菜，又叫苦苣菜，是一种具有药用价值的野生植物，多生长在川谷、山陵、道旁。多被做成凉菜，其味新鲜爽口，清凉嫩香，营养丰富。

"祭三车"

小满时节，在我国江南一带有"祭三车"的民俗活动。"三车"，指水车、油车和丝车。

这时候，南方早稻追肥、中稻插秧，水源要有基本保证。旧时候水车是重要的灌溉工具，祭祀水车，寄寓的是人们对丰收的期望。

这时候，南方的油菜籽成熟了，为了在榨油的过程中多出油、出好油，人们也会举行祭祀榨油车的活动。

这时候，蚕茧结成，正待采摘缫丝，南方一带也会举行祭蚕仪式，希望能够多产丝。

"满"字是形声字,表示充实、充满的意思。《说文解字》释"满"为"盈溢也"。

·小满时节,农作物生长到了什么阶段?

8. Grain Buds

Grain Buds, the eighth solar term, is in the last ten days of May.

👁 Seeing

During these days, the wheat and other grain plants in the North turn to be mature and the harvest time is coming. It becomes rainy in the South.

👂 Listening

"Now I know in a cage of gold, she never sang so sweet, as when she roamed freely in the woods." Summer is the time for the thrush to reproduce. During this time, the loud and melodious sound of the thrush is attractive.

👃 Smelling

Around this solar term, a lot of flowers is blooming in the North. The flowers of jujube trees are an important source of honey. The honey picked during this period is good and is favored by honey lovers.

👄 Eating

Herba ixeris is a kind of vegertables which is fresh, rich of nutrition and has the heat removal function.

🖐 Touching

There is an activity called "worshipping three cars" in many areas during this solar term. The three cars are a waterwheel, an oil tanker and a textile car.

The rice should be fertilized in the South China, so the water should be ganranteed. The waterwheel was an important irrigation tool in ancient China, and worshipping the waterwheel was a blessing form for plenty of water.

At this time, the southern rapeseeds are mature.In order to increase oil in the process of oil extraction, people will also have an activity to worship the oil tankers.

It's also time for the silkworms to make cocoons, and the ceremony of worshipping the textile car will be held in the South, hoping to get a good harvest.

9·芒种

每年六月上旬进入芒种，芒种是二十四节气中的第九个节气。

视

有芒之种谷可稼种矣。螳螂生，鵙始鸣，反舌感阳而发，遇微阴而无声也。

——《月令七十二候集解》

52

螳螂（táng láng）：也称刀螂，一种昆虫，全身呈绿色或土黄色，体长，腹部肥大，头三角形。捕食害虫，有益农业，属益虫。

鵙（jú）：古人称为伯劳鸟，性凶猛，喜食昆虫、蛙类。

反舌无声：有多种解释，一般认为反舌是一种鸟，称为反舌鸟，因为感受到了阴气，而停止了鸣叫。

芒种的"芒"字，是指麦类等有芒植物即将开始收获；芒种的"种"字，是指谷黍类作物播种的节令，所以，"芒种"也称为"忙种""忙着种"，是古时候一年中农民最忙的季节。

芒种前后，中国长江中下游地区开始进入多雨的梅雨季节。

听 伯劳鸟鸣

"东飞伯劳西飞燕，黄姑织女时相见。"伯劳与燕子都是候鸟，每年会在固定的日子飞到一定的地方生活。伯劳东飞去，燕子西飞去，就是劳燕分飞、关系破裂的意思。黄姑是牛郎，传说与织女相爱，但是每年只能见一次面。

嗅 芒种花

芒种花也叫金丝梅、金丝桃，大多生长在南方地区，在芒种期间开花，还具有药用价值。

梅子

芒种期间是梅子成熟的时节。不过，新鲜的梅子往往十分酸涩，无法直接吃，需要进行加工，古代有"青梅煮酒论英雄"的典故。

送花神

芒种之后，部分鲜花开始陆续凋谢了，于是，古代文人雅士会摆设礼物，为"花神"饯行。

《红楼梦》里提道："那些女孩子们，或用花瓣柳枝编成轿马的，或用绣锦纱罗叠成干旄（máo）旌（jīng）幢（chuáng）的，都用彩线系了。每一棵树上，每一枝花上，都系了这些物事。满园里绣带飘飘，花枝招展。"轿、马是为花神准备的交通工具；干是盾牌；旄、旌、幢是不同的旗子。

"芒"字是形声字，上边为"艹"，为形旁，下边为"亡"，为声旁，《说文解字》曰："芒，草端也。"

- "芒种"的"芒"是指什么？

9. Grain in Ear

Grain in Ear, the ninth solar term, is in the first ten days of June.

👁 Seeing

The name of this solar term means all the grain with ears, including the wheat will have a harvest and it's also the time to sow the seeds of the millet valley corps. It's the busiest time of the year.

Around this solar term, the lower reaches of the Yangtze River have begun to enter the rainy season of Huangmei.

👂 Listening

People can hear the singing of the shrike.

👃 Smelling

hypericum patulumor is grown mostly in South China and blooms this time. It has medicinal value.

👄 Eating

The plum is mature in this period, but the fresh plums are very sour and can't be eaten directly. They need to be processed.

✋ Touching

After this solar term, all kinds of flowers begin to fade. And so it's an ancient custom for the literati to hold a farewell party for the flowers.

10. 夏至

每年六月下旬进入夏至，夏至是二十四节气中的第十个节气。

视

至，极也。万物于此皆假大而至极也。鹿角解，蜩始鸣，半夏生。

——《月令七十二候集解》

鹿角解：是指此时开始收割鹿角。

蜩（tiáo）：蝉。

半夏：又名地文、守田等，广泛分布于中国长江流域以及东北、华北等地区。因为其生于夏至前后，故得名"半夏"。

夏至日是我国白天最长、夜晚最短的一天。夏至前后天气很热，然而还到最热的时候。俗话说："冷在三九，热在三伏。"夏至之后，才开始"入伏"，炎热会慢慢到来。

蝉鸣

　　唐代虞世南写过一首名为《蝉》的诗："垂緌（ruí）饮清露，流响出疏桐。居高声自远，非是藉秋风。"从夏至开始，蝉鸣的声音便开始伴随着暑热，一直持续到秋天。

半夏花

　　半夏花，不仅可以观赏，还具有药用功效。

凉面

俗语说："吃过夏至面，一天短一线。"夏至时节北方人喜欢吃面。这时候吃面，人们喜欢用凉水过一遍，因为这时候天气炎热，凉面可以降温开胃。

夏至以后，白天开始变短。古时候的人白天做针线活，由于白天变短，故每天能做的针线活也少了，此所谓"一天短一线"。

冬病夏治

按照中医理论，夏至阳气最盛，人的机体经络顺畅，适宜在夏季进行治疗，可以提高机体的抗病能力，这是中医学"天人合一""未病先防"疾病预防观的体现。

"至"在《说文解字》中释为"鸟飞从高下至地也"。象形字，后引申为"到来"的意思。

· 夏至为什么不是最热的时候？

· 你见过一边有太阳一边下雨的现象吗？为什么这种现象大多在夏季出现？

10. Summer Solstice

夏长

Summer Solstice, the tenth solar term, is in the last ten days of June.

👁 Seeing

On the Summer Solstice the day time is the longest for the whole year in the northern hemisphere. The temperatures become higher around the Summer Solstice. After the Summer Solstice, the hottest days of the year comes, which is called the "the dog days".

👂 Listening

Peole can hear the cicadas during this period.

👃 Smelling

Pinellia ternata can be used not only for viewing but also for medicinal value.

👄 Eating

During these days, people like to eat the cold noodles. Because It is very hot and the cold noodles can make people feel cool and it's good for health,too.

After the Summer Solstice, the day time begins to shorten.

✋ Touching

According to the traditional Chinese medicine, Yang is the highest durig these days,and the body function is also the best. Health care in summer can improve the body's disease resistance. It is the traditional Chinese medicine concept— "prevention before disease".

11·小暑

每年七月上旬进入小暑，小暑是二十四节气中的第十一个节气。

视 👁

暑，热也，就热之中分为大小，月初为小，月中为大，今则热气犹小也。温风至，蟋蟀居壁，鹰始击。

——《月令七十二候集解》

解读

　　小暑时节，天气炎热。之所以称为"小暑"，是寓意更热的天气还在后边。在小暑期间，我国南方炎热多雨，北方也即将进入汛期，农作物生长迅速，人们大都躲在家里，不愿意出门。

听

蟋蟀

"蟋蟀独知秋令早，芭蕉正得雨声多。"当听到蟋蟀声的时候，天气虽然仍旧炎热，但是秋天已经不远了。

嗅

石竹

唐代诗人独孤及在一首诗中称赞石竹说："不怕南风热，能迎小暑开。"优雅的石竹正当夏秋少花的季节开放，能为生活增添别样的趣味。

西瓜

　　消暑的水果，莫过于西瓜。西瓜之名带有"西"字，一说是古人认为西瓜是从西域传来的。明代科学家徐光启的《农政全书》记载："西瓜，种出西域，故之名。"

消暑

　　炎炎夏日，古人是怎么消暑的呢？唐代白居易写过一首《消暑》："何以消烦暑，端坐一院中。眼前无长物，窗下有清风。散热由心静，凉生为室空。此时身自保，难更与人同。"可见，心平气和也是古人消暑的重要门径。

"暑"和"热"意思接近，但又略有分别。"暑"主要表达湿的含义，"热"则表达燥的含义。

· 汉语中的暑和热，表达的意思有什么区别？

· 夏季的暴雨有什么危害？

11. Minor Heat

Minor Heat, the eleventh solar term, is in the first ten days of July.

👁 Seeing

During these days, it is very hot. Minor means the hotter weather is still behind. It's hot and rainy in South China and it will turn to rainy days in North China. The corps grow quickly and people tend to stay at home for avoiding the hot weather outside.

👂 Listening

People can hear the sound of cricket at this time. It means the autumn will come.

👃 Smelling

There aren't many blooming flowers at this time but the dianthus, which adds a different flavour to life.

👄 Eating

Nothing more than the watermelon can reduce the heat in summer.

✋ Touching

How does the ancient people reduce the heat and keep cooler in summer? Keeping a calm mood is an improtant way.

12·大暑

每年七月下旬进入大暑，大暑是二十四节气中的第十二个节气。

视

腐草为萤，土润溽暑，大雨时行。

——《月令七十二候集解》

70

注解

腐草为萤：萤火虫卵最初寄生于腐烂的草中。

溽（rù）：湿。

解读

　　大暑是一年中最热的时期，农作物生长最快，大部分地区下雨很多，但是长江中下游地区经常出现"伏旱"，旱、涝灾害也经常出现。

雨声

夏季的雨，迅疾而猛烈，正是"前日看花心未足，狂风暴雨忽无凭。"

荷花

"接天莲叶无穷碧，映日荷花别样红。"这是古人对荷花的描述。亭亭荷花在一汪碧水中散发着沁人清香，使人心旷神怡。

绿豆汤

《随息居饮食谱》："绿豆甘凉，煮食清胆养胃，解暑止渴。"炎炎夏日，绿豆汤是最佳解暑饮品。

数伏

俗话说："冷在三九，热在三伏。"小暑前后开始"入伏"，也称为"数伏"，表示热气"伏"在其中。"数伏"分为初伏、中伏、末伏。其中初伏从夏至后第三个庚日算起，共10天，中伏在初伏之后，一般持续10—20天，末伏是自立秋后的第一个庚日起，共10天。

中国古代有一种"干支纪年法"，用"十天干"（甲、乙、丙、丁、戊、己、庚、辛、壬、癸）和"十二地支"（子、丑、寅、卯、辰、巳、午、未、申、酉、戌、亥）相配组合成60组，周而复始。

表： 干支排列表

01 甲子	11 甲戌	21 甲申	31 甲午	41 甲辰	51 甲寅
02 乙丑	12 乙亥	22 乙酉	32 乙未	42 乙巳	52 乙卯
03 丙寅	13 丙子	23 丙戌	33 丙申	43 丙午	53 丙辰
04 丁卯	14 丁丑	24 丁亥	34 丁酉	44 丁未	54 丁巳
05 戊辰	15 戊寅	25 戊子	35 戊戌	45 戊申	55 戊午
06 己巳	16 己卯	26 己丑	36 己亥	46 己酉	56 己未
07 庚午	17 庚辰	27 庚寅	37 庚子	47 庚戌	57 庚申
08 辛未	18 辛巳	28 辛卯	38 辛丑	48 辛亥	58 辛酉
09 壬申	19 壬午	29 壬辰	39 壬寅	49 壬子	59 壬戌
10 癸酉	20 癸未	30 癸巳	40 癸卯	50 癸丑	60 癸亥

"伏"由"人"和
"犬"组成，表示狗服从
于人，引申为趴下、屈服
等意思。

- 夏天消暑的饮品有哪些？
- 夏季为什么不能吃过多寒凉的食品？

12. Major Heat

Major Heat, the twelveth solar term, is in the last ten days of July.

👁 Seeing

Major Heat means the hottest days in a year. The corps are growing quickly and it rains a lot in most places of China. But in the middle and lower reaches of the Yangtze River, there is always a "drought" in the dog days. Drought and flood disasters often occur.

👂 Listening

The rain in summer often comes quickly and heavily.

👃 Smelling

In summer, the lotus exudes refreshing fragrance in the green water, which can make pople feel fresh.

👄 Eating

Mungbean soup, sweet and cool, is a popular drink to reduce the heat in summer.

✋ Touching

The dog days comes these days, before or after the Minor Heat. The dog days are about forty days and they are the hottest days in summer.

秋夕

杜牧

银烛秋光冷画屏，轻罗小扇扑流萤。

天阶夜色凉如水，卧看牵牛织女星。

秋收

13·立秋

每年八月上旬进入立秋，立秋是二十四节气中的第十三个节气。

视 👁

秋，揫也，物于此而揫敛也。凉风至，白露降，寒蝉鸣。

——《月令七十二候集解》

注解

掎（jiū）：聚集。

解读

　　立秋意味着暑去秋来，也意味着庄稼成熟，收获的季节到了。立秋之后，早晚便能感受到丝丝凉意了。

秋雨声

　　"雨声飕（sōu）飕催早寒，胡雁翅湿高飞难。"春雨和秋雨不同，春雨大多是绵绵细雨，带来的是暖意，而秋雨则是"一场秋雨一场寒"。秋雨来了，带来的是凉意。

芝麻开花

　　俗话话："芝麻开花，节节高。"北方的芝麻在立秋前后开花，一节节长高，结出芝麻。

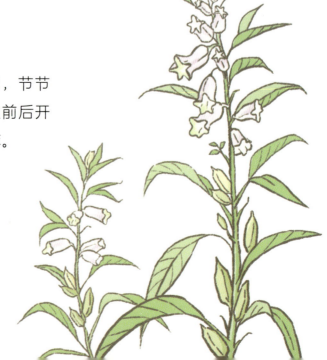

水果

　　立秋前后，各类水果陆续成熟，市面上售卖的水果品类十分丰富，这是一个收获的季节。

贴秋膘

　　"苦热恨无行脚处，微凉喜到立秋时。"在古代，人们在立秋这天会称一下体重，并与立夏时的体重值进行对比。夏天的几个月，天气炎热，人们没有食欲，吃的清凉寡淡，体重自然会减轻。立秋以后逐渐转凉，人们胃口渐开，遂把这期间吃好吃的称为"贴秋膘"。

"秋"字为形声字，由"火"与"禾"组成，表示庄稼成熟。

· 春雨和秋雨带给人的感受，有什么区别？

· 扇扇子为什么能使人凉快？

13. Start of Autumn

Start of Autumn, the thirteenth solar term, is in the first ten days of August.

👁 Seeing

This solar term means the summer is going and the autumn is coming. The corps are ripe and the harvest time is up. During this period, it's still hot but a few days later, it will become cooler and people can feel the coolness. After this solar term, the sound of the cicada is as loud as in summer.

👂 Listening

The rain in spring is different from the rain in autumn. It drizzles a lot in spring and it brings warmness, while the rain in autumn brings the coolness.

👃 Smelling

The sesame blossoms around this porid.

👄 Eating

During these days, the litchi, pineapple, longan in the south, and the apricot,peach, pear and apple in the north tend to be ripe one after another. There are a lot of fruits on the markets and the harvest days are coming.

✋ Touching

In ancient time, it's a custom to weigh on this day and compare the weight with that on Start of Summer. In the hot summer, people eat less, so they lose weight; while in autumn, It is cool and people's appetite is great.

14·处暑

每年八月下旬进入处暑，处暑是二十四节气中的第十四个节气。

视

处，止也。暑气至此而止矣。鹰乃祭鸟，天地始肃，禾乃登。

——《月令七十二候集解》

注解

鹰乃祭鸟：古人认为鹰是义鸟，因为它捕到猎物后会先放着，像人用餐前要祭祀一样；而且，它不捕捉有孕的动物，所以认为它"义"。

解读

　　处暑节气，炎热开始退去，大部分地区雨季也行将结束，秋高气爽的天气即将来到，田里的庄稼将陆续收获。

秋声

古人对秋天的声音有深切的感悟。宋代欧阳修所写的《秋声赋》中说："初淅沥以萧飒，忽奔腾而砰湃，如波涛夜惊，风雨骤至。其触于物也，鏦（cōng）鏦铮铮，金铁皆鸣；又如赴敌之兵，衔枚疾走，不闻号令，但闻人马之行声。"你在秋天听到了哪些声音呢？

桂花

处暑时节，桂花开放，香气扑鼻，令人神清气爽。"人闲桂花落，夜静春山空。"古人留下了许多描写桂花的佳句，你还能举出一两个吗？

酸梅汤

　　"处暑酸梅汤，火气全退光。"清凉爽口的酸梅汤是夏日消暑的良品，在中国已经有几百年的历史。清朝郝懿行在《都门竹枝词》中写下："铜碗声声街里唤，一瓯（ōu）冰水和梅汤。"生动地反映了当时酸梅汤在民间广受欢迎的情景。

拜土地神

　　处暑之后，庄稼陆续成熟，很多地方会举行祭拜土地神的仪式，表达对土地的感谢。很多人在处暑当天下地干活后并不洗手，直到第二天才洗，以表示珍惜土地。

知 💡

"处"字是形声字，繁体字作"處"，异体字作"处"。"处"由"几""夂"两部分组成，表示人的脚步停留在"几"旁，也就是桌子旁边，引申为停止的意思。

- 在秋天，你听到了哪些声音呢？
- 处暑的"处"是什么意思？

14. End of Heat

End of Heat, the fourteenth solar term, is in the last ten days of August.

Seeing

At this time, the heat begin to fade, and the rainy days will end in most areas. People will see the high and blue sky soon. The corps in the field have been harvested.

Listening

There are many poems describing the sound of autumn. Do you hear those voices in autumn?

Smelling

During these days, the osmanthus blossoms and brings fragrant air to people. There are many poems about the osmanthus. Can you say out one or two sentences?

Eating

It has about hundreds of years' history to drink the syrup of plum in summer. The soup is sweet and sour, which can reduce the heat.

Touching

After this solar term, all kinds of corps are mature both in the South and the North. In many places, people hold a ceremony to worship the land gods for their bless and the people don't wash their hands affer farmwork utill the next day in order to express their cherishness to the land.

15. 白露

每年九月上旬进入白露，白露是二十四节气中的第十五个节气。

视 👁

秋属金，金色白，阴气渐重，露凝而白也。鸿雁来，元鸟归，群鸟养羞。

——《月令七十二候集解》

注解

元鸟归：元鸟，指燕子。归，指燕子由北方飞回南方。

养羞：储存过冬的食物。

解读

"蒹葭（jiān jiā，即芦苇）苍苍，白露为霜。"白露时节，天气开始转凉，白天和夜晚的温差加大，清晨能在叶子上发现有许多露珠，凉爽的秋天正当其时。

雁鸣

白露过后，秋意渐浓，候鸟开始南迁，在郊外的天上，能看到雁阵，听到"嘎—嘎—"的叫声。

月季

月季原产于中国，为常绿灌木，叶为羽状复叶，花期很长，花色较多。后来，月季传入欧洲，经过培育杂交之后形成很多品种。

龙眼

　　福州有"白露必吃龙眼"的习俗。龙眼，即桂圆，有较好的药用价值。此时期的龙眼个大味甜口感好，所以白露吃龙眼是再好不过的了。

祭禹王

　　大禹是治水的英雄，生活在太湖地区的渔民称他为"水路菩萨"。每年白露，这里都要举行较大规模的祭禹王的香会，以寄托人们对美好生活的祈盼。

"露"字是象形字，由形旁"雨"和声旁"路"组成。露水是靠近地面的水蒸气，在夜间遇冷凝结成的小水球。

- 芦苇生长在什么环境下？
- 秋天的露珠是怎么形成的，为什么秋季容易形成露珠？

15. White Dew

秋收

White Dew, the fifteenth solar term, is in the first ten days of September.

👁 Seeing

When White Dew comes, it indicates the beginning of cool autumn. The temperature declines gradually and the vapors in the air often condence into white dew on the grass and trees at night. The cool autumn is at the right time.

👂 Listening

When it turns cold, the migratory birds begin to fly to the south. Rows of wild geese can be seen in the countryside's sky and their "zha - zha" sound can be heared .

👃 Smelling

The Chinese roses originat in China and the flowers can bloom for a long time. Later, the Chinese roses were introduced into Europe, and many varieties were cultivated after cross breeding.

👄 Eating

It's a custom to eat longan in Fuzhou area. Longan is good for people's health. It can nourish the blood, calm the nerves, and improve one's looks. The longan at this time is big, sweet and tastes great.

✋ Touching

White Dew is the time for people in the Taihu Lake area of East China to offer sacrifices to Da Yu, a hero who tamed floods.

16. 秋分

每年九月下旬进入秋分，秋分是二十四节气中的第十六个节气。

视

雷始收声，蛰虫坏户，水始涸。

——《月令七十二候集解》

96

注解

坏：音péi，陶瓦之泥曰坏，细泥也。

解读

　　秋分这一天，昼夜时间均等，秋分之后，中国便开始进入昼短夜长的日子了。这时候天气干燥，降水不多，不过每一次降水，都意味着一次冷空气的到来，开始一步步走进深秋。

溪水声

　　"水落溪声壮，天寒山色奇。"秋日的山林，景色怡人，随着山势的起伏，溪水声时缓时急。

枇杷花

　　秋分前后，百花凋谢，枇杷花却坚强地盛开着，颜色鲜艳诱人，正如古人所描述的"山枇杷，花似牡丹殷泼血"。

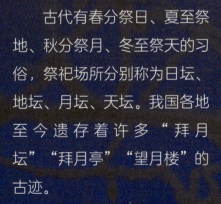

味

螃蟹

俗话说："西风响，蟹脚痒。"秋分时节，是蟹肉最肥美的时候。《红楼梦》里，史湘云在"藕香榭"大摆螃蟹宴，薛宝钗在席间赋出了"眼前道路无经纬，皮里春秋空黑黄"的描述螃蟹的诗。

触

祭月

古代有春分祭日、夏至祭地、秋分祭月、冬至祭天的习俗，祭祀场所分别称为日坛、地坛、月坛、天坛。我国各地至今遗存着许多"拜月坛""拜月亭""望月楼"的古迹。

"月"字是象形字，像一个半月的形状。秋分时，我国大部分地区秋高气爽，气温适宜，晚上月明星稀，是赏月的最佳时刻。

· 为什么秋分前后最适合吃螃蟹？

· 秋分的"分"是什么意思？

16. Autumn Equinox

Autumn Equinox, the sixteenth solar term, is in the last ten days of September.

👁 Seeing

On the day of Autumn Equinox, the daytime is equal to the night time, and after this day, the daytime will be shorter and the nighttime will be longer in China. It's dry and rains less.

👂 Listening

When the water falls, along with the ups and downs of the mountains, giving out different tones of slowness and urgency.

👃 Smelling

During the days, a lot of flowers begin to fall, except the bright loquat flower.

👄 Eating

Its time to eat the crab. In the famous book *The Dream of Red Mansions*, it describes the lively scene of eating crabs.

✋ Touching

It's a custom to worship the moon.

17. 寒露

每年十月上旬进入寒露，寒露是二十四节气中的第十七个节气。

露气寒冷，将凝结也。鸿雁来宾，雀入大水为蛤，菊有黄华。

——《月令七十二候集解》

注解

蛤（gé）：水生软体动物。古人误以为秋冬飞向大海的鸟变成了蛤蜊。

解读

　　寒露时的气温比白露时更低，露水就要凝结成霜。寒露到，意味着秋季正式开始，东北、西北则进入深秋。

秋虫叫

　　唐代诗人张仲素写过一首《杂曲歌辞·秋夜曲》："丁丁漏水夜何长，漫漫轻云露月光。秋壁暗虫通夕响，寒衣未寄莫飞霜。"漫漫秋夜，计时的漏壶响着"丁丁"的滴水声，暗处伴随着各种无名草虫的叫声，不同的声音构成了这一时节大自然的交响曲。

木芙蓉

　　芙蓉，原产我国，因其花晚秋始开，霜侵露凌却丰姿艳丽，因而又名"拒霜花"。苏轼有诗云："千林扫作一番黄，只有芙蓉独自芳。唤作拒霜知未称，细思却是最宜霜。"

柿子

俗语说："立秋核桃白露梨，寒露柿子红了皮。"

柿子是成熟较晚的水果，在深秋的薄暮中，远远望去，柿子挂满枝头，像一个个小红灯笼，格外喜气。

斗蟋蟀

蟋蟀也叫促织、蛐蛐儿。斗蟋蟀是一项古老的娱乐活动，是中国民间搏戏之一，兴起于唐代，盛行于宋代，至今仍十分流行。

知

“寒”字的组成十分复杂，外面是“宀”（mián，即房屋），中间是“人”，人的左右两边是四个“草”，指很多“草”，下面的“仌”（两点水，bīng）指“冰”，表示人踡曲在室内以草避寒，天气很冷的意思。

· 为什么在天气转凉时，花儿逐渐凋谢？

17. Cold Dew

Cold Dew, the seventeenth solar term, is in the first ten days of October.

👁 Seeing

The temperature at this time are much lower than that in White Dew. Dew can condense into frost these days. The autumn officially arrives. In the northeast and northwest, it has entered the late autumn.

👂 Listening

The night time is longer and longer and the sound of the insects break its quietness. Different sounds can be heared in the night and they makes a symphony of nature at this time of the season.

👃 Smelling

Hibiscus flowers bloom in late autumn. They have bright colors and don't be fear of the frost.

👄 Eating

The persimmon is mature in late autumn. People can see that persimmons are covered with branches, like red lanterns.

✋ Touching

The sound of the cricket means the autumn is coming. Cricket fight is an ancient entertainment and still popular nowadays after thousands of years.

107

18. 霜降

每年十月下旬进入霜降，霜降是二十四节气中的第十八个节气。

视 👁

气肃而凝，露结为霜矣。豺祭兽，草木黄落，蛰虫咸俯。

——《月令七十二候集解》

豺**祭兽**：豺狼将捕获的猎物陈列后再食用。

　　霜降时节，我国北方地区气温降低，出现白霜，树叶枯黄落下，各种昆虫开始准备过冬。

听

落叶

　　唐代白居易的《秋月》写道："落叶声策策，惊鸟影翩（piān）翩。"在深秋的树林里，万籁俱寂，能听到簌簌的落叶声。

嗅

菊花

　　菊花往往开于百花凋谢之后，其独立的品格深受历代人士的喜爱。在中国传统文化中，菊花具有吉祥、长寿之意。东晋的陶渊明爱菊成癖，留下"采菊东篱下，悠然见南山"等名句。菊花也是饮品，《神农本草经》记载："菊花久服能轻身延年。"

萝卜

　　俗语说："处暑高粱白露谷，霜降到了拔萝卜。"又说："冬吃萝卜夏吃姜，不劳医生开药方。"秋冬季节，天气干燥，萝卜具有顺气、消滞、生津、解毒的作用，宜于在此季节食用。

赏红叶

　　"远上寒山石径斜（xiá），白云生处有人家。停车坐爱枫林晚。霜叶红于二月花。"杜牧的《山行》写出了作者对深秋红叶的喜爱。深秋时节，枫树、栎树的叶子开始由绿渐变成红黄色，漫山遍野的红叶，成为这个时节最为壮丽的景观。

"霜"字是象形字，由"雨"和"相"组成，本义指气温降到摄氏零度以下时，近地面空气中水汽的白色结晶。

- 中国人为什么对菊花情有独钟？
- 霜和露有什么区别？

18. Frost's Descent

秋收

Frost's Descent, the eighteenth solar term, is in the last ten days of October.

👁 Seeing

During this time of the year, the temperature continues to decrease and people can see the white frost in the early morning. The leaves begin to turn yellow and fall down. All kinds of insects prepare for the hiberation.

👂 Listening

In the late autumn, everything is silent in the woods, and you can even hear the sound of falling leaves.

👃 Smelling

The chrysanthemum is the iconic flower of Cold Dew. Its independent character is cherished by people. In traditional Chinese culture, the chrysanthemum has the meaning of good luck and longevity. There are many poems praising the chrysanthemum in the history.

👄 Eating

It is dry in autumn.While the radish has much water in it, and is very suitable for eating in autumn.

✋ Touching

In late autumn, the leaves of the maple and the oak begin to turn yellow and red all over the mountains, which becomes the most magnificent landscape this season.

白梅

王冕

冰雪林中著此身，不同桃李混芳尘；

忽然一夜清香发，散作乾坤万里春。

冬藏

19. 立冬

每年十一月上旬进入立冬，立冬是二十四节气中的第十九个节气。

视 👁

冬，终也，万物收藏也。水始冰，地始冻，雉入大水为蜃。

——《月令七十二候集解》

雉入大水为蜃：雉，野鸡；蜃，蛤。立冬后，野鸡一类的大鸟不多见了，而海边却可以看到外壳与野鸡的线条与颜色极相似的大蛤，故古人认为雉到立冬后便变成蛤了。

立冬时节，秋季作物收晒完毕，收藏入库，人们呆在室内，动物也蛰伏起来，准备迎接寒冷冬天的到来。

寒鸦

　　"荒山野水照斜晖，啄雪寒鸦趁始飞。"越是寒冷的时节，人们越能听到寒鸦的鸣叫声，这是冬日特有的声音。

饺子

　　饺子是极具中国特色的食品。据传饺子为"医圣"张仲景首创，他将羊肉和一些祛寒药材放在锅里煮熟，再捞出来切碎，用面皮包成耳朵状，称"娇耳"，人们吃了之后，可以抵御伤寒，渐渐地，在冬季吃饺子成为习俗。

触

冬藏

　　《史记》中说："春生夏长，秋收冬藏，此天道之大经也。"人类的身体也应该顺应大自然的变化之道，入冬天之后，便开始养精蓄锐、休养生息。此时，养生的核心不止是物质上的滋补，更重要的是精神上的"内敛宁静"，避免不必要的"肝火"。

"冬"字由"夊"（zhōng、"终"的意思）与"仌"组成，表示天寒地冻的时候，一年到了终点，即为冬。

- 中国民间以立冬为冬季的开始，为什么？
- 农谚"立冬阴，一冬温；立冬晴，一冬凌"是什么意思？

19. Start of Winter

Start of Winter, the nineteenth solar term, is in the first ten days of November.

👁 Seeing

Start of Winter means winter is coming and crops harvested in autumn should be stored up, some animals prepare for hiberate.

👂 Listening

People can hear the crows in cold winter. This is the special sound in winter.

👄 Eating

Jiaozi is a native food in China. There is a legend about it, Jiaozi is passed down by "Medical Saint" Zhang Zhongjing. He cooked mutton, hot peppers and herbs to dispel the cold and increase body heat. He wrapped these ingredients into a clough skin and made them into an ear shape. Since then, people have learned to make the food which is known as "Jiao zi".

✋ Touching

It's the natural rule to become alive in spring, grow in summer, harvest in autumn and store in winter. We should obey the rule in order to keep healthy. The most important thing is to keep a calm mood.

20·小雪

每年十一月下旬进入小雪，小雪是二十四节气中的第二十个节气。

视 👁

雨下而为寒气所薄，故凝而为雪。小者，未盛之辞。虹藏不见，天气上升，地气下降，闭塞而成冬。

——《月令七十二候集解》

闭塞：古人认为天空中的阳气应该向下，大地的阴气应该向上，形成交汇，天地相通。而从小雪开始，阴阳二气相分离，天地不通，故称"闭塞"。

自小雪始，进入隆冬时节。万物失去生机，北方一般不再下雨，而开始下雪。

寒风声

　　唐代诗人元稹在《咏廿四气诗·小雪十月中》写道："满月光天汉，长风响树枝。"北方的冬天，光秃秃的树干在寒冷的北风的吹动下，"吱吱"作响，这是北方冬日特有的声音。

酸菜

　　酸菜是日常生活中常见的开胃小菜，最初是为了延长蔬菜的保存时间。在我国，制作酸菜拥有悠久的历史。东汉许慎《说文解字》提到："菹（zū）菜者，酸菜也。"《齐民要术》里则详细记载了酸菜的制作方法。

收白菜

　　俗话说："入冬萝卜小雪菜。"小雪前后是白菜收获的季节。在物资匮乏的年代，中国北方地区都会冬储大白菜。

125

"雪"字由"雨"和"彐"组成。在温度低于零度时,降水会在空中凝结成冰晶落下,即为雪。

· 小雪这天一定会下雪吗?节气小雪和天气预报的小雪有什么区别?

· 你知道有哪些描写下雪的诗歌?

20. Minor Snow

冬藏

Minor Snow, the twentith solar term, is in the last ten days of November.

◉ Seeing

It begins to enter the midwinter after the Minor Snow. All things lose their vitality, and the trees in the North only have branches. It does not rain any longer, and the snow comes.

⌒ Listening

In the North, the bare trunk Creaks when the cold wind comes, which is a peculiar sound of winter in the north.

⌒ Eating

The pickled Chinese cabbage is an appetizer in daily life. It's made originally to extend the preservation. Thousands of years ago, the book *QiMinYaoSu* introduces the method of making pickled Chinese cabbages.

⋔ Touching

For the Chinese, the cabbage is a populer vegetable in winter. During the days around the Minor Snow, people begins to collect cabbages, which is cheap but nourishing.

21·大雪

每年十二月上旬进入大雪，大雪是二十四节气中的第二十一个节气。

大者，盛也。至此而雪盛矣。鹖鴠不鸣，虎始交，荔挺出。

——《月令七十二候集解》

128

注解

鹖鴠（hé dàn）：一种像野
鸡的鸟，俗称寒号鸟。

荔：即马薤（xiè）。

解读

　　大雪前后，由于气温很低，北方
的降雪会长时间不融化。这时候，万
物蛰藏，一片万籁俱寂的景象。

野鸡鸣

野鸡又名山鸡、七彩锦鸡，多栖息于灌丛与草地中，在迫不得已时会起飞，边飞边发出"咯咯"的叫声。

腊肉

俗话说："小雪腌菜，大雪腌肉。"大雪前后，很多家里开始腌制腊肉。一般来说，腊肉制作完成之后，新年就快到了。

赏冰灯

　　晶莹剔透的冰灯是冬日里别有韵味的景致。制作冰灯古已有之，清朝十分重视冬天的冰戏活动。

　　去看一次冰灯，并且了解一下冰灯的制作过程吧。

　　"冰"字由"仌"和"水"组成。更早时候，"冰"字只有左半部分，水变成冰以后，体积会增大，表面上涨，也就是"仌"上拱结构的来源。

· "冬天麦盖三层被，来年枕着馒头睡"，大雪和丰收有什么关联呢？

21. Major Snow

Major Snow, the twenty-first solar term, is in the first ten days of December.

👁 Seeing

During Major Snow, the snow begins to accumulate on the ground. The temperature drops significantly. At this time, there is a scene which is quiet and still.

👂 Listening

Pheasants has strong cold resistance. Up to now, in winter, the occasional "giggle" of the pheasant can still be heard in the wild shrubs.

👄 Eating

Major Snow is the time to make the perserved bacon. After finishing making the perserved bacon, the New Year is coming.

✋ Touching

The sparkling ice lantern is a unique scenery of winter. Making Ice lantern has a long history. The royal family in Qing Dynasty, whose comes from the Northeast of China, attaches great importance to the winter ice play activities.

Please go to see an ice lantern show and try to learn how to make the ice lantern.

22·冬至

每年十二月下旬进入冬至，冬至是二十四节气中的第二十二个节气。

视 👁

终藏之气，至此而极也。蚯蚓结，麋角解，水泉动。

——《月令七十二候集解》

注解

蚯蚓结：蚯蚓处在蜷缩状态。

麋（mí）角解：古人认为麋与鹿不同，麋属阴，冬至以后阴气开始退去，阳气开始生发，因此冬至以后麋退角。

解读

　　冬至是我国白天时间最短的一天，过了冬至，白天便开始一点点变长。古人认为，冬至是阴阳消长的时节。不过，冬至夜意味着阴气极盛而阳气极衰，此间积累的寒气会使冬至以后的天气变得更加寒冷。

麻雀

麻雀是中国最常见，分布最广的鸟类，以谷物为食。寒冷的冬日里，麻雀小巧的身影、"叽喳"的叫声，平添了几分生气。

馄饨

馄饨在南方一些地区也被称为"云吞""抄手"。过去北京有"冬至馄饨夏至面"的说法。《燕京岁时记》载："夫馄饨之形有如鸡卵，颇似天地混沌之象，故于冬至日食之。""馄饨"与"混沌"谐音，所以民间将吃馄饨引申为打破混沌，开辟天地，这是对冬至的美好希望。

数九

人们常用"数九寒天"来表述冬季。《数九歌》一直在我国北方广为流传：

一九二九不出手；三九四九冰上走；

五九六九沿河看柳；七九河开八九雁来；

九九加一九，耕牛遍地走。

"数九"指从冬至当天算起，每九天算一"九"，一直数到"九九"八十一天，"九尽桃花开"，天气就暖和了。

在古代，生产力十分落后，缺乏有效的取暖设备，寒冷的冬天十分难熬，而"九"是最大的个位数，以"九"为单位象征着普通百姓眼里漫长的冬日，"数九"有掐着日子盼望春天到来的意味。

尝试制作一幅九九消寒图

《说文解字》说九字"象其屈曲究尽之形",是个位数最大的数。古人认为,"冬至次日,数及九九八十一日为寒尽"。

· 制作一个九九消寒图。

· 我国南北方的冬天有哪些不同?

22. Winter Solstice

冬藏

Winter Solstice, the twenty-second solar term, is in the last ten days of December.

Seeing

Winter Solstice has the shortest day time in China. After this day, the daytime becomes longer. The Winter Solstice also marks the arrival of the coldest season in the year.

Listening

Sparrow is the most common and widely distributed bird in China. Their small shape and sound add more vitality to the winter.

Eating

It's also a custom to eat wonton on this day. Wonnton represents people's good wishes for the Winter Solstice.

Touching

From the Winter Solstice, each nine days is a "nine cold days",utill the ninth nine days, namely 81 days altogether. After these 81 days, the warm days will come.

23·小寒

每年一月上旬进入小寒，小寒是二十四节气中的第二十三个节气。

视

月初寒尚小，故云，月半则大矣。雁北乡，鹊始巢，雉始雊。

——《月令七十二候集解》

雉：雉在中国出现的很早，在两千多年前的《诗经》中便提到"雄雉于飞，上下其音。"后来，雉成为很多鸟类的统称。此处指野鸡。

雊（gòu）：叫。

小寒时节，正是数九隆冬，北方各地十分寒冷。

喜鹊声

"小寒连大吕，欢鹊垒新巢。"黑白相间的喜鹊有着美丽的身姿。"喜鹊声喈喈，俗云报喜鸣。"在寒冷的冬日，尤其是我国的北方。

喜鹊"喳喳"的声音可以给寂静的冬日带来一些活力。

水仙花

水仙在我国有上千年的栽培历史。宋代诗人刘克庄这样描述水仙花："岁华摇落物萧然，一种清风绝可怜。不俱淤泥侵皓素，全凭风露发幽妍。"

在严寒的冬日里，芳香的水仙花常常成为一道别样的风景。

腊八粥

农历腊月初八，我国各地都有吃腊八粥的习俗。《燕京岁时记》载："腊八粥者，用黄米、白米、江米、小米、菱角米、栗子、红江豆、去皮枣泥等，合水煮熟，外用染红桃仁、杏仁、瓜子、花生、榛穰、松子及白糖、红糖、琐琐葡萄，以作点染。"

腊祭

农历的十二月之所以被称为"腊月"，是因为在这个月要进行腊祭。腊祭，曾经是一年中最隆重的祭祀活动之一。

"腊"字最初可能表示打猎的意思，将打猎得来的动物用于祭祀祖先和众神，祈求来年五谷丰登、平安吉祥，便是腊祭的主要活动内容。

"冷"字是形声字，由形旁"仌"和声旁"令"组成，《说文解字》记："冷，寒也。"

- 小寒有三候：雁北乡，鹊始巢，雉始雊，这是什么意思？
- 文人墨客为什么多吟咏梅花？

23 Minor Cold

Minor Cold, the twenty-third solar term, is in the first ten days of January.

👁 Seeing

During Minor Cold, the bitter cold stage of winter comes in most areas.

👂 Listening

In the cold winter, there are some kinds of birds which people can see especiallly in the north, including the magpie. In Chinese traditional culture, magpie symbolizes luck. People will be very happpy to hear the Sound of magpie.

👃 Smelling

Narcissus has been grown in China for thousands of years. In cold winter days, the narcissus often becomes a different scenery.

🍷 Drinking

Moderate Cold is often in the twelfth lunar month. On the 8th day of the twelfth month in Chinese calendar, it's a custom to drink Laba porridge. This porridge is made by eight kinds of nuts and fruits, namely yellow rice, rice, glutinous rice, millet, water chestnuts and so on.

🤚 Touching

The twelfth month in Chinese calander is also called layue, because people always hold one of the most important worship activities this month ."La" means hunting originally and people use the animals and food which they hunted for the sacrifice, hoping a good harvest in the next year.

24．大寒

每年一月上旬进入大寒，大寒是二十四节气中的第二十四个节气。

视 👁

鸡乳育也，征鸟厉疾，水泽腹坚。

——《月令七十二候集解》

注解

鸡乳育：可以孵小鸡。

厉疾：处在捕食能力很强的状态。

水泽腹坚：水中的冰一直冻到中央。

 解读

　　大寒表示寒冷的程度更深，是一年中最寒冷的时候。

147

鸡鸣狗吠

　　"鸡鸣高树巅,狗吠深宫中。"这是传统社会最常见的景象。大寒过后,气温即将回暖。在寒冷的冬日,听到母鸡"咯咯咯"的觅食声,能让人感到由衷地温暖。

山茶花

　　大寒时节,山茶花迎寒而开。山茶又名耐冬,其坚韧耐寒、执着奔放的品格一直为古人青睐。宋代诗人陆游曾写诗描写山茶花:"雪裹开花到春晚,世间耐久孰如君?"范成大也写诗:"门巷欢呼十里村,腊前风物已知春。"

年糕

　　过年前后，各地都有吃年糕的习俗。年糕与"年年高"谐音，预示着人们的生活一年比一年高，所以广受欢迎。

　　各地的年糕有多种做法，你能说出来几种呢？

除旧迎新

　　大寒时节，往往与岁末重合，全国各地都处在辞旧迎新的氛围中。家家户户都在忙着赶集置办年货、写春联，准备过新年。

"岁"字的繁体写法是"歲",由"步"和"戌"（xū）组成。有人认为，这表示一个人从"戌"月走过了一年，到了下一个"戌"月。古人使用十二地支表示一年的十二个月，"戌"表示十一月，是旧历法中一年的开端。

· 在我国南方广大的地区，为什么有大寒吃糯米的习俗？

· 大寒到春节期间，民间有哪些民俗活动？

24. Major Cold

Major Cold, the twenty- fourth solar term, is in the first ten days of January.

 Seeing

Major Cold means the coldest days in the year is coming.

Listening

Major Cold is the coldest days in winter. In other words, the warm days is not far. During these days, a hen can lead a flock of chicks and "giggle" for food, which can make people feel warm.

Smelling

The camellia flowers open these days. Their cold-tolerance and unrestrained character is appreciated by the ancients.

Eating

It's a custom to eat rice cakes during these days. In Chinese, rice cakes means better and better, so they are loved by people all over the country.

Touching

This solar term is always at the end of a year. So there is an atmosphere of sending the past year and welcoming the new year. There is no farm work at this time and people are busy preparing for the New Year.

后　记

　　本书为面向小学阶段的儿童读物，也可用于课堂教学。在经过多次讨论后，本书最终采用最具直观性的"五感"，即眼、耳、鼻、舌、身所代表的视觉、听觉、嗅觉、味觉、触觉来呈现每个节气的典型特征；本书的英文部分并不严格对译，只做一般性介绍。

　　其中，视觉选择主题意象，听觉选择风雨声、鸟鸣声，嗅觉选择节令花卉（冬季的部分节气未安排此部分），味觉选择节令食品，触觉则依据不同节令的典型特征，分别选择节令民俗、养生、人伦等相关活动。此外，每个节气还选择了一个相应的汉字作为"知觉"部分，以凸显中国文化的特征。这种形式能让人直观感受到节气的变化，体味到中国人的时间观念，也与小学生的认知能力相吻合。

　　节气作为一种文化体系，在中国历史上经历了长久的积累，体现了中国人的文化观与时间感，是中国人生活方式的反映，也是中国人生命观的象征。在寒来暑往、秋收冬藏的往复循环中，一辈又一辈的中国人一点一点感受着天地之气的来往，一圈一圈增进着自己的生命印记，在二十四节气的年轮之下，不断探寻着天地变化与人类生活的关系，将中国文化从往古的岁月中推向未来。

　　过去，节气曾与农业社会的结构相与为一，并在此基础上形成了复杂的文化体系。在进入城市化时代之后，传承节气文化需要从新时期出发，因为这不仅是在追寻一种历史的记忆，更是为了构筑跨越时空的中国文化印记，丰富当代人的生活感受。基于此，也出于对课时容量的考虑，本书对于各节气的五感，均只选择了一个最具典型性的点作为内容，这当然无法全面地反映广袤国土上无比丰富的节气文化。我们需要理解，学习节气文化不仅仅是为了学习很多历史与民俗常识，也是为了"自我"文化意识的唤醒。

　　如用于课堂教学，学校可以选择安排在小学阶段的某一年度，按照节气的顺序逐课组织教学活动，每一种节气使用一课时的时间。

编者